Contents

T0385892

How to be a times tables detective!

Times tables are full of patterns and connections. If you know these, it will help you to remember the times tables. It will also help you to use the tables to solve problems and to reason about numbers. There are detectives in this book who will help you to spot patterns. They will also sometimes ask a question to challenge you. When you spot a detective, take the chance to think in a bit more depth, and become a times tables detective!

T Circle every multiple of 3 on the number track.

Count on in 3s from 0.

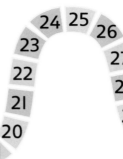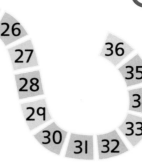

S Fill in the missing numbers to complete the pattern.

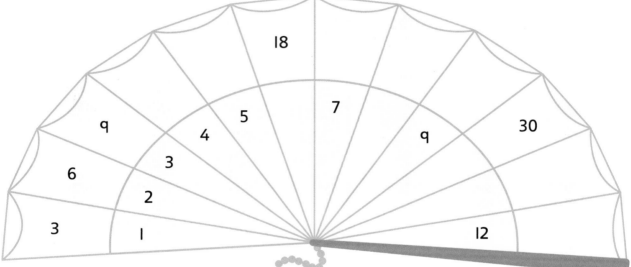

18

5   7

9   4   9   30

3

6

2

3   1   12

D Join each frog to the correct lily pad.

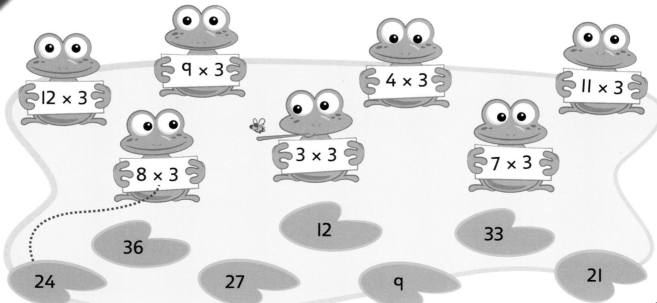

9 × 3

4 × 3   11 × 3

12 × 3

8 × 3   3 × 3   7 × 3

12   33

36

24   27   9   21

Fill in the missing multiples of 3.

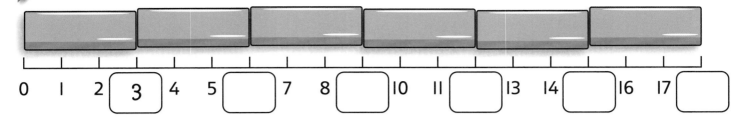

0   1   2   3   4   5   ☐   7   8   ☐ 10 11 ☐ 13 14 ☐ 16 17 ☐

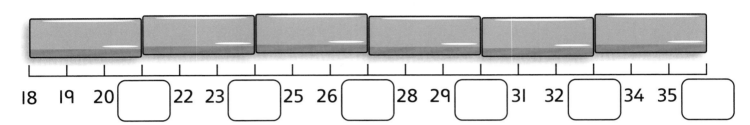

18 19 20 ☐ 22 23 ☐ 25 26 ☐ 28 29 ☐ 31 32 ☐ 34 35 ☐

 Each rod is worth 3. Write the value of each set of rods.

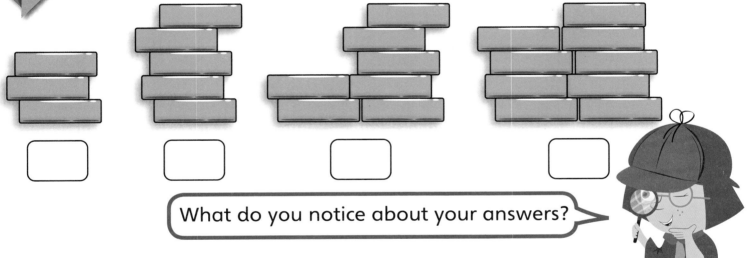

☐   ☐   ☐   ☐

What do you notice about your answers?

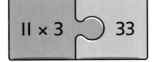 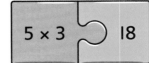 

Which of these are wrong? Correct any mistakes you see.

| 7 × 3 ⊃ 21 | 11 × 3 ⊃ 33 | 5 × 3 ⊃ 18 | 8 × 3 ⊃ 27 |

| 4 × 3 ⊃ 12 | 9 × 3 ⊃ 24 | 12 × 3 ⊃ 24 | 6 × 3 ⊃ 15 |

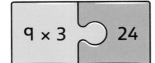 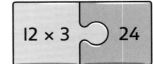

5

Circle the correct number of dice to match the number of dots to the number below.

Count in 3s.

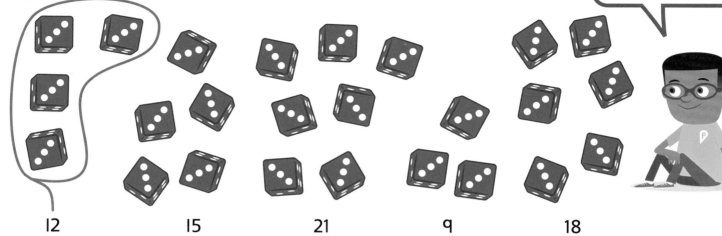

| 12 | 15 | 21 | 9 | 18 |

Write a ×3 fact to match the number of dots on each set of dice.

$\boxed{3}$ × 3 = $\boxed{9}$

$\boxed{}$ × 3 = $\boxed{}$

$\boxed{}$ × 3 = $\boxed{}$

$\boxed{}$ × 3 = $\boxed{}$

$\boxed{}$ × 3 = $\boxed{}$

$\boxed{}$ × 3 = $\boxed{}$

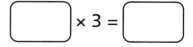

Choose two numbers from 1 to 6. Add the numbers together and multiply the total by 3. Fill in the table. Repeat with a different pair of numbers each time.

	Pair 1	Pair 2	Pair 3	Pair 4	Pair 5	Pair 6	Pair 7	Pair 8
1st number	1							
2nd number	5							
Total	6							
Total × 3	18							

Do you think you can make all the multiples of 3 up to 36?

More multiples of 3

 Colour the multiples of 3 in this grid.

1	2	3	4	5	6	7	8	9	10
11	12	13	14	15	16	17	18	29	20
21	22	23	24	25	26	27	28	29	30
31	32	33	34	35	36	37	38	39	40

What pattern can you see made by the multiples of 3?

Draw lines to join each plug to its matching socket.

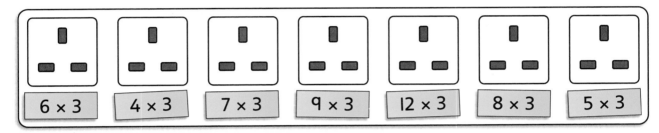

| 6 × 3 | 4 × 3 | 7 × 3 | 9 × 3 | 12 × 3 | 8 × 3 | 5 × 3 |

| 21 | 18 | 27 | 12 | 36 | 15 | 24 |

Find the answers to the multiplications. Use the answers to draw the mole's route across the mole hills to the other side.

4 × 3
1 × 3
6 × 3
9 × 3
7 × 3
5 × 3
12 × 3
2 × 3
8 × 3
11 × 3
10 × 3
3 × 3

7

Time to divide

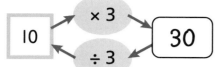 Write a ×3 and a ÷3 fact for each diagram.
Fill in any missing numbers.

10 → ×3 → 30
10 ← ÷3 ← 30

☐ × 3 = ☐
☐ ÷ 3 = ☐

7 → ×3 → ☐
7 ← ÷3 ← ☐

☐ × 3 = ☐
☐ ÷ 3 = ☐

 9 → ×3 → ☐
9 ← ÷3 ← ☐

☐ × 3 = ☐
☐ ÷ 3 = ☐

 Divide each number by 3.

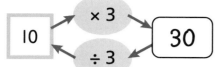

Multiply your answer by 3 to check.

 30 ☐    15 ☐    9 ☐    36 ☐

24 ☐   33 ☐   18 ☐   27 ☐

Look at the number being divided and
the answer. Do you see a pattern?
Think about odd and even numbers.

 Fill in the missing numbers.

5 × 3 = ☁   12 × 3 = ☁   9 × 3 = ☁

☁ × 3 = 12   ☁ × 3 = 24   ☁ × 3 = 3

33 ÷ 3 = ☁   21 ÷ 3 = ☁   30 ÷ 3 = ☁

☁ ÷ 3 = 9   ☁ ÷ 3 = 3   15 × 3 = ☁

Bar patterns

 ×3

T Colour in the rest of the bar chart for the ×3 table.

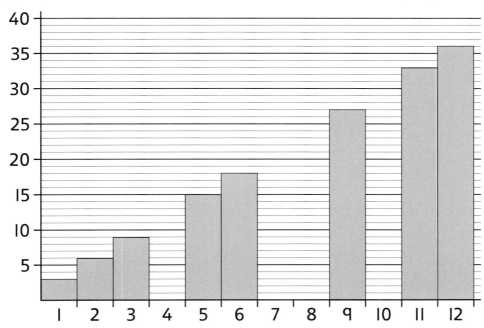

S Answer these questions about the bar chart above.

How many sections tall is the 6 × 3 bar? _____

How many less than 30 is 9 × 3? _____

Which bar is 15 sections tall? _____

How many more is 12 × 3 than 6 × 3? _____

Find the difference between 11 × 3 and 9 × 3. _____

D Use the clues to find the answers. Write each answer as a multiplication and as a number.

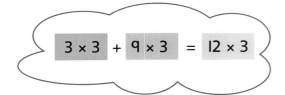

3 × 3 + 9 × 3 = 12 × 3

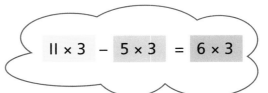

11 × 3 − 5 × 3 = 6 × 3

1 The sum of 4 × 3 and 8 × 3. _____

2 The difference between 12 × 3 and 7 × 3. _____

3 The sum of 7 × 3 and 8 × 3. _____

4 The difference between 20 × 3 and 9 × 3. _____

×3 puzzles

Fill in the missing numbers. Then colour all the even numbers.

Do you notice a pattern with odd and even multiples of 3?

3	6	I2			24			36

Write how many threes make each number.

24 — 8 threes   18 — threes

I5 — threes   27 — threes

9 — threes   33 — threes

30 — threes   2I — threes

Use the clues to find the answers. Every answer is a multiple of 3.

- More than I5
- Less than 8 × 3
- Even [ ]

- Less than 27
- Greater than 6 × 3
- Odd [ ]

- Less than I5
- Greater than I × 3
- Odd [ ]

- Less than 32
- Greater than 7 × 3
- Odd [ ]

- More than I2
- Less than 8 × 3
- Even [ ]

- Less than 37
- Greater than 9 × 3
- Odd [ ]

T Circle groups of stars in two different ways in each pair of arrays to show the multiplication.

Group the first one in 3s.

12 = 4 × 3

15 = 5 × 3

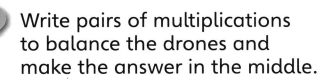

 S Write pairs of multiplications to balance the drones and make the answer in the middle.

When multiplying, numbers can be in any order and the answer will be the same.

8 × 3   **24**   3 × 8

× 3   **18**   3 ×

× 3   **12**   3 ×

× 3   **36**   3 ×

× 3   **27**   3 ×

× 3   **21**   3 ×

 **D** How many ×3 facts can you find using the cards? You can use cards more than once.

_____

_____

_____

| × | = | 1 | 2 |

| 3 | 4 | 7 |

Word puzzles

 **T** Write the answers in digits.

What are eight 3s? `24`

Multiplying 7 by 3 gives what answer? ☐

What is 9 times 3? ☐

33 is made from how many 3s? ☐

Find 6 multiplied by 3 ☐

Dividing 36 by 3 gives what answer? ☐

 S Write a calculation to help you answer each problem.

36 children get into 3s. How many groups are there?

How many legs do 10 three-legged aliens have?

_____   _____

 D Write a word problem for each multiplication and answer it.

8 × 3   27 ÷ 3

_____   _____

_____   _____

_____   _____

_____   _____

Forward to 4s

T Each chair has 4 legs. Each stack has one more chair than the one before. How many legs are in each stack of chairs?

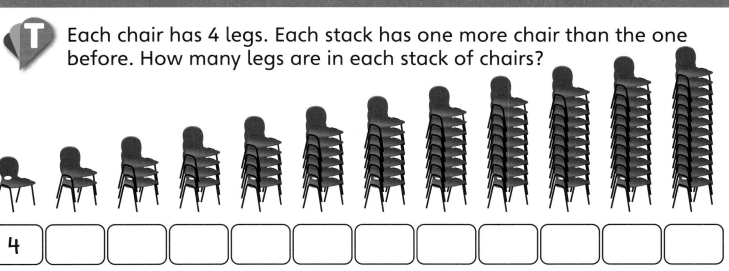

| 4 | | | | | | | | | | | |

Can you see a pattern? Are the answers odd or even?

S Write the answer at the end of each length of wool.

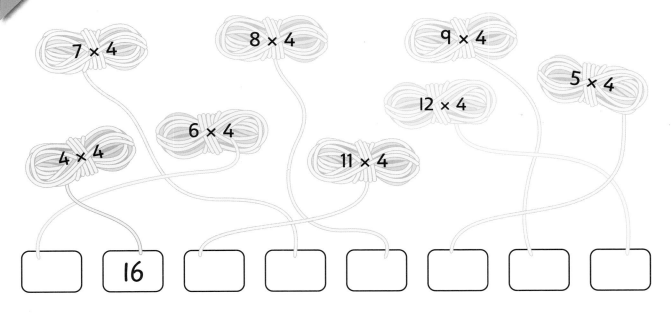

7 × 4   8 × 4   9 × 4   5 × 4   12 × 4   6 × 4   4 × 4   11 × 4

| | 16 | | | | | | |

D Join together pairs that have the same product. Write a multiplication for the sock that doesn't have a match.

9 × 4   3 × 4   8 × 4   6 × 4   10 × 4   11 × 4   7 × 4

6 × 2   12 × 2   4 × 9   4 × 11   4 × 8   8 × 5   _____

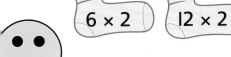

13

T Write two multiplication facts for each array.

The first array is 2 rows of 4 or 4 columns of 2.

$$\boxed{2} \times \boxed{4} = \boxed{}$$

$$\boxed{} \times \boxed{} = \boxed{}$$

$$\boxed{} \times \boxed{} = \boxed{}$$

$$\boxed{} \times \boxed{} = \boxed{}$$

S Draw an array of dots to show each pair of facts. Fill in the missing numbers.

$3 \times 4 = 12$

$4 \times 3 = 12$

$5 \times 4 = 20$

$4 \times 5 = \boxed{}$

$4 \times 7 = \boxed{}$

$\boxed{} \times 4 = \boxed{}$

D Find the answers to the multiplications to fill in the crossword. Write one digit in each white square

Across	Down
1 3 × 4	1 4 × 3
2 7 × 4	2 4 × 6
3 11 × 4	3 4 × 10
4 5 × 4	4 4 × 7
6 12 × 4	5 4 × 8
7 8 × 4	6 10 × 4
8 4 × 4	7 9 × 4

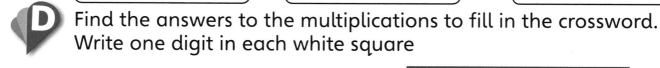

Along the right line

T Draw lines to match each card with its correct position on the number line. Write the answers below the number line.

| 3 × 4 | 4 × 4 | 7 × 4 | 9 × 4 | 11 × 4 |

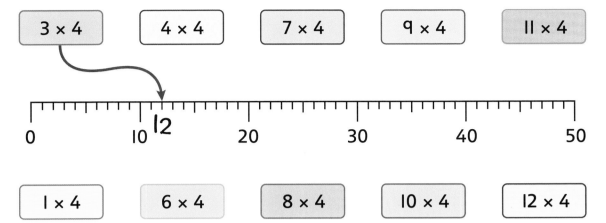

0   10   12   20   30   40   50

| 1 × 4 | 6 × 4 | 8 × 4 | 10 × 4 | 12 × 4 |

S This is a coded message. Colour the letters of the multiples of 4 to find out what the message says.

22	41	44	34	18	25	12	38	6	31	26	14	32
S	T	E	A	M	I	N	G	A	H	E	A	D

28	13	7	24	34	6	36	42	38	14	15	16	20	4	1
O	N	A	F	A	S	T	R	A	I	N	H	E	L	P

8	6	21	22	11	38	40	31	48	33	18	26	35
I	T	I	S	D	A	N	G	E	R	O	U	S

Message: _____

D Choose multiples of 4 to write some ÷4 facts.

Write the multiple of 4 first. Divide it by 4 and give the answer.

_____   _____

_____   _____

_____   _____

4-legged friends

T Puppies have 4 legs. Write how many legs there would be in each basket.

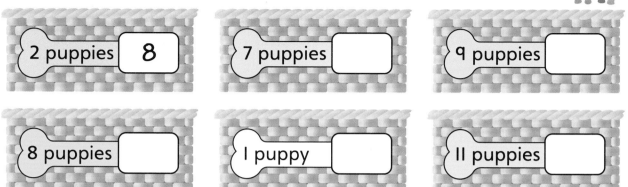

2 puppies | 8
7 puppies |
9 puppies |
8 puppies |
1 puppy |
11 puppies |

S A bag of dog food costs £4. How many bags can you buy with each amount of money?

= £10   = £5   = £2   = £1

5

D Write the multiples of 4 in order from 4 to 48.

Look at the ones digit of the multiples. Can you see any patterns? What do you think the answer to 13 × 4 will be?

16

Feeling sheepish

T Write two multiplication facts to show how many sheep are in each question.

Count how many groups of 3 or 4.

4	×	3	=	

	×		=	

3	×	4	=	

	×		=	

What do you notice about the two facts for each question?

S Answer the questions in order, from left to right, top row first. Use the answers to plot the sheep's path to the other side of the field.

3 × 4   4 × 4   4 × 6   5 × 4   4 × 9   10 × 4
4 × 2   7 × 4   11 × 4   4 × 1   4 × 6   12 × 4

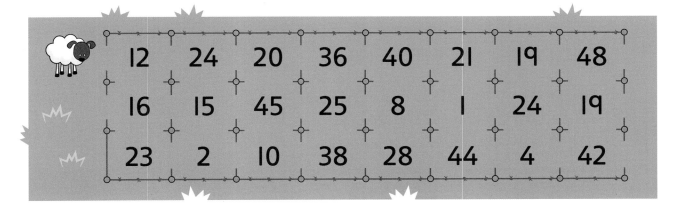

12	24	20	36	40	21	19	48
16	15	45	25	8	1	24	19
23	2	10	38	28	44	4	42

D Put a tick if the two answers are the same in each pair. Put a cross if they are different.

4 × 10	10 × 4 ☐	1 × 4	4 × 1 ☐	4 × 6	6 × 5 ☐
11 × 4	4 × 11 ☐	4 × 2	2 × 4 ☐	5 × 4	4 × 5 ☐
12 × 4	4 × 12 ☐	8 × 2	8 × 4 ☐	9 × 4	4 × 9 ☐

Double double

 Use 'double, double' to multiply each number by 4.

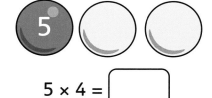
Double the number, then double the answer.

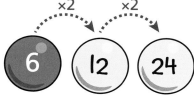

6 × 4 = [24]

5 × 4 = [ ]

7 × 4 = [ ]

12 × 4 = [ ]

 Fill in the empty spaces. Choose a multiple of 4 from the outer circle. Use 'halve and halve again' to divide each number by 4.

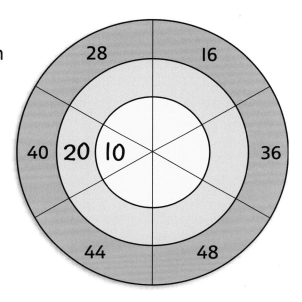

 Write the answers. Do you see a pattern?
Use it to work out 20 × 4.

5 × 2 = [ ]

6 × 2 = [ ]

8 × 2 = [ ]

11 × 2 = [ ]

5 × 4 = [ ]

6 × 4 = [ ]

8 × 4 = [ ]

11 × 4 = [ ]

20 × 4 = [ ]

Bingo 4s

×4

 T Write a ×4 fact and a ÷4 fact using each set of numbers.

> For ÷4 facts the multiple of 4 will come first.

24
6   4
_____
_____

44
4   11
_____
_____

28
4   7
_____
_____

36
9   4
_____
_____

S Do the multiplications and colour in the answers on the bingo cards. Work from left to right along the top row, then the bottom row. Which bingo card gets 3 in a line first?

| 20 ÷ 4 | 6 × 4 | 10 × 4 | 36 ÷ 4 | 7 × 4 |

| 8 × 4 | 24 ÷ 4 | 11 × 4 | 16 ÷ 4 | 12 × 4 |

0	5	30
28	50	4
9	35	24

15	6	9
40	18	48
3	44	32

40	6	34
1	7	28
5	4	35

 D The numbers on the first bingo card are 4 times the numbers on the second. Fill in the missing numbers.

12	28	40	32
	48	4	
	36	24	

		7	
5			11
2			4

8s are great

T Each brown rod is 8 units long. Fill in the missing multiples of 8.

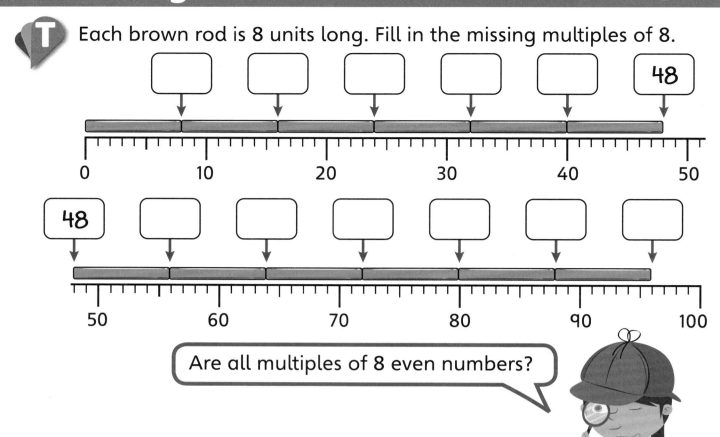

Are all multiples of 8 even numbers?

S Each rod is worth 8. Fill in the table.

Number of rods	2	4	3	6	5	7	10	12	8	9
Multiple of 8	16									

D Put a tick if the number is a multiple of 8. Put a cross if it is not.

Watch out. Not every even number is a multiple of 8!

48 ✓	30	56
44	32	88
40	54	31
38	74	76
64	72	96

Write the correct multiplication for each array. What do you notice?

$3 \times 2 = 6$ $3 \times 4 = 12$ $3 \times 8 = \boxed{}$

$\boxed{} \times \boxed{} = \boxed{}$ $\boxed{} \times \boxed{} = \boxed{}$ $\boxed{} \times \boxed{} = \boxed{}$

Write the answers. Do you see a pattern?

$4 \times 2 = \boxed{}$ $7 \times 2 = \boxed{}$ $8 \times 2 = \boxed{}$ $9 \times 2 = \boxed{}$

$4 \times 4 = \boxed{}$ $7 \times 4 = \boxed{}$ $8 \times 4 = \boxed{}$ $9 \times 4 = \boxed{}$

$4 \times 8 = \boxed{}$ $7 \times 8 = \boxed{}$ $8 \times 8 = \boxed{}$ $9 \times 8 = \boxed{}$

 Use 'double, double, double' to multiply each number by 8.

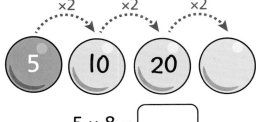

$5 \times 8 = \boxed{}$

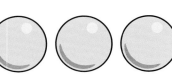 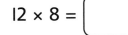

$12 \times 8 = \boxed{}$

$15 \times 8 = \boxed{}$

 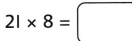

$21 \times 8 = \boxed{}$

T Count on in 8s from 0. Fill in the boxes.

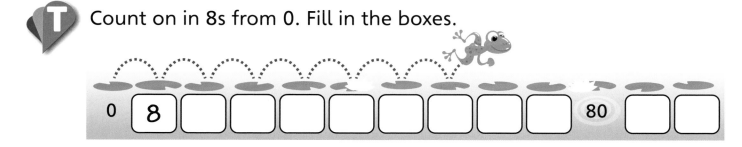

0 | 8 | | | | | | | | 80 | |

S Draw a path from one side of the stones to the other. Use only multiples of 8.

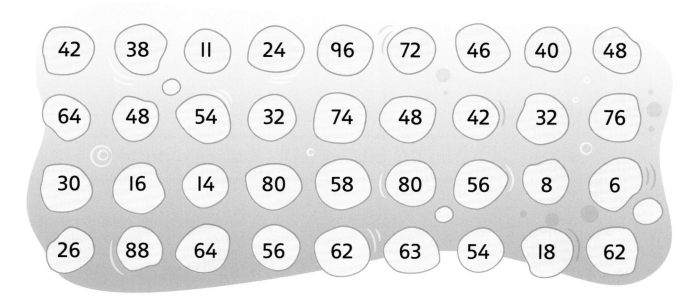

42	38	11	24	96	72	46	40	48
64	48	54	32	74	48	42	32	76
30	16	14	80	58	80	56	8	6
26	88	64	56	62	63	54	18	62

D Choose two numbers from the hopscotch track. Multiply them both by 8 then add the multiples together. How many ways can you make 96?

10

8   9

7

5   6

4

2   3

1

_____

_____

_____

Can you see a quick way to do this?

Colour the multiples of 8 in this grid.

Is every multiple of 8 even? _____

Is every even number a multiple of 8? _____

1	2	3	4	5	6	7	8	9	10
11	12	13	14	15	16	17	18	19	20
21	22	23	24	25	26	27	28	29	30
31	32	33	34	35	36	37	38	39	40
41	42	43	44	45	46	47	48	49	50
51	52	53	54	55	56	57	58	59	60
61	62	63	64	65	66	67	68	69	70
71	72	73	74	75	76	77	78	79	80

What do you notice about all the multiples of 8?

 Write true or false next to each scroll.

All multiples of 8 are multiples of 4. _____

All multiples of 4 are multiples of 8. _____

The sum of the digits of a multiple of 8 is always even. _____

All multiples of 8 end in 0, 2, 4, 6 or 8. _____

There are 5 multiples of 8 between 20 and 60. _____

 Use the clues to solve the puzzles. The answers are all multiples of 8. Make up a puzzle for a partner to solve.

I am between 60 and 70. _____

The sum of my digits is 12. _____

If you double me you get 144. _____

 _____

T Fill in the missing input and output numbers.

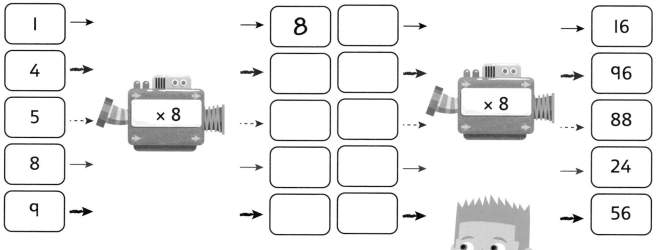

1	→		→	8		→		→	16
4								96
5	×8					×8		88
8								24
9								56

To find output numbers, multiply by 8.
To find input numbers, divide by 8.

S Fill in the missing numbers in the octagons. The first one has been done for you. Then write a ×8 fact and a ÷8 fact using the numbers in each octagon.

Octagon 1: 8   9   72

Octagon 2: 7   8

Octagon 3: 1   8

Octagon 4: 8   12

_____ _____ _____ _____

_____ _____ _____ _____

D Fill in the missing numbers.

$48 \div 8 = \boxed{}$ $40 \div 8 = \boxed{}$ $\boxed{} \div 8 = 10$

$\boxed{} \div 8 = 12$ $8 \div \boxed{} = 1$ $\boxed{} \div 8 = 7$

$72 \div 8 = \boxed{}$ $\boxed{} \div 8 = 11$ $160 \div 8 = \boxed{}$

8-legged friends

 Wolf spiders have 8 eyes. Complete the tables.

Number of wolf spiders	1	2	3	4	5	6
Number of eyes	8	16				

Number of wolf spiders	7	8	9	10	11	12
Number of eyes						

 Fill in the missing numbers in the spiders' webs.

16   8   3   40
     2   5
   12   7
     6   9

     16   88
96   2   8
   32   72
     48   56

Multiply inner numbers by 8 to get outer numbers.
Divide outer numbers by 8 to get inner numbers.

 Join pairs of cards whose products add up to 104. What pattern do you notice?

 4 × 8

3 × 8

7 × 8

 9 × 8

11 × 8

5 × 8

6 × 8

2 × 8

8 × 8

10 × 8

There are four different types of hen on a farm. Each day the hens double the number of eggs they laid the day before. Fill in the missing numbers.

Double the previous number in each column.

Monday	3	4	6	9
Tuesday	6			
Wednesday	12			

 Multiply each tractor number by 2, 4 and 8 to find the number of hay bales.

× 2 =

× 4 =

× 8 =

× 2 =

× 4 =

× 8 =

 What word is hidden in the grid? Colour each number that is **not** a multiple of 8 to find out.

42	28	44	8	66	78	26	56	20	84	28
54	8	80	72	90	32	4	64	22	72	30
18	34	84	56	14	12	46	16	82	42	26
22	88	16	80	24	40	68	72	96	48	100
26	76	66	88	22	30	52	8	44	38	78

Lots of tables

 Fill in the missing numbers to complete the grids.

×	2	10	5
4	8		
7		70	
12			

×	3	4	8
6	18		
11			88
8			

Multiply the numbers on the left by each number at the top.

 Work out all the missing numbers in these grids.

×	4		8
	24		48
9		45	
		20	

×	10	3	
		18	48
			24
7	70		

Be careful! There may be more than one way to make a multiple.

 Complete the grids in three different ways. Which of your grids has the most numbers that are greater than 60?

×			
	24		
		36	
			20

×			
	24		
		36	
			20

×			
	24		
		36	
			20

Join sacks with the same answer. Not all sacks have a match.

8 ÷ 4   12 × 5   12 × 3   8 × 5   10 ÷ 5   8 × 3

3 × 12   5 × 8   5 ÷ 10   3 × 8   4 ÷ 8   5 × 12

> Careful! Numbers can be in any order when multiplying, but not when dividing.

S Write whether the answers to each pair of calculations are 'the same' or 'different'. Write what the answers are.

4 × 3) 3 + 3 + 3 + 3   5 × 4) 4 × 5

_____   _____

12 × 10) 6 × 5 × 5   8 × 5 × 2) 8 × 10

_____   _____

4 + 4 + 4) 3 + 3 + 3 + 3   9 × 4) 8 × 3

_____   _____

D Put a tick next to the correct answers. Put a cross next to any wrong answers and write the correct answers.

7 × 5 × 2 = 70 ☐   3 × 3 × 4 = 36 ☐

2 × 2 × 2 × 3 = 18 ☐   4 × 3 × 2 = 14 ☐

3 × 2 × 4 = 24 ☐   8 × 8 × 1 = 64 ☐

2 × 4 × 7 = 56 ☐   4 × 10 × 8 = 320 ☐

Fill in the multiplication grids.

×	2	3	4	5	8	10
1						
2						
3						
4						
5						
6						

×	2	3	4	5	8	10
7					56	
8						
9						
10						
11						
12						

Tell a partner about any patterns you used.

 Fill in the missing numbers.

$48 \div 4 = \boxed{}$ $16 \div 8 = \boxed{}$ $45 \div 5 = \boxed{}$

$48 \div \boxed{} = 6$ $16 \div \boxed{} = 4$ $27 \div \boxed{} = 9$

$\boxed{} \div 8 = 7$ $\boxed{} \div 5 = 12$ $21 \div \boxed{} = 7$

 Choose one number from each tray. Write a correct division sentence with the numbers. Cross off each number as you use it. You should be able to make six division sentences.

| 30, 32, 33, 36, 40, 48 | 3, 4, 5, 8, 8, 10 | 4, 4, 6, 6, 9, 11 |

Put a **circle** around multiples of 3. Draw a **square** around multiples of 4. Draw a **triangle** around multiples of 8.

8 (9) 10 11 12 13 14 15 16 17 18 19 20

21 22 23 24 25 26 27 28 29 30 31 32 33

Which number has all three shapes? _____

Think of a larger number that would have all three

shapes. _____

 Find the number in these puzzles.

An odd multiple of 3
Not a multiple of 4
More than 27
Less than 7 × 5 [ ]

A multiple of 8
Not a multiple of 5 or 6
More than 24
Less than 10 × 5 [ ]

 Write a division by 3, 4, 5 or 8 to give a whole number answer.

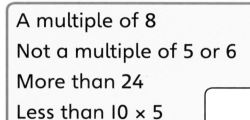
Think about which times tables the first number appears in.

27 ÷ [ ] = [ ]   35 ÷ [ ] = [ ]

36 ÷ [ ] = [ ]   64 ÷ [ ] = [ ]

28 ÷ [ ] = [ ]   96 ÷ [ ] = [ ]

45 ÷ [ ] = [ ]   21 ÷ [ ] = [ ]